HOUGHTON MIFFLIN HARCOURT

Texas
JOURNEYS

Program Authors

James F. Baumann · David J. Chard · Jamal Cooks
J. David Cooper · Russell Gersten · Marjorie Lipson
Lesley Mandel Morrow · John J. Pikulski · Héctor H. Rivera
Mabel Rivera · Shane Templeton · Sheila W. Valencia
Catherine Valentino · MaryEllen Vogt

Consulting Author
Irene Fountas

HOUGHTON MIFFLIN HARCOURT
School Publishers

Hello, Reader!

Think about all of the stories you have read. Which one is your favorite so far?

In this book, you will meet characters who help their friends, work hard at school, and solve mysteries. You will even read about a soccer player that you may know. Whatever they do, the characters in these stories always try their best.

Do your best as you read. You will learn even more words!

Sincerely,

The Authors

Three Cheers for Us!

Big Idea Always try your best.

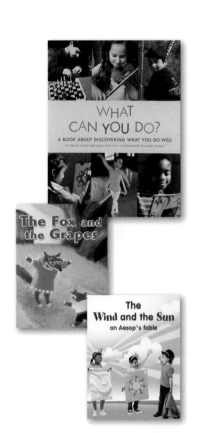

Three Cheers for Us!

Unit 6

Big Idea

Always try
your best.

Selections

Lesson 26

✓ **WORDS TO KNOW**
HIGH-FREQUENCY WORDS

teacher

studied

surprised

toward

bear

above

even

pushed

Vocabulary Reader   Context Cards

TEKS 1.3H identify/read high-frequency words; **ELPS** 1F use accessible language to learn new language; 3B expand/internalize initial English vocabulary

10

Words to Know

Read Together

● Read each Context Card.

● Choose two blue words. Use them in sentences.

1

teacher

The art teacher shows how to use a brush.

2

studied

She studied the flower before she drew it.

3

surprised

He was surprised to see such a big statue.

4

toward

He walked slowly toward the art table.

5

bear

The picture of the bear looks very real.

6

above

These shapes hang high above the floor.

7

even

This box has even more crayons in it.

8

pushed

He pushed the clay into new shapes.

Background

✓ **WORDS TO KNOW**   **Art Class**   The art teacher pushed the cart of art supplies toward the children.   They studied how to use them.   A boy drew a bear.   A girl drew the sun above tall trees.   The class even surprised their teacher by painting a class picture!

Art Supplies

crayons

paintbrush

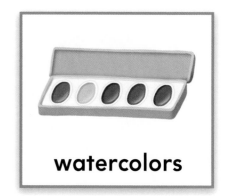

watercolors

markers

paper

Name some other art supplies.

TEKS 1.4C establish purpose/monitor comprehension; **RC-1(A)** establish reading purposes; **ELPS 1E** internalize new basic/academic language; **2G** understand meaning/main points/details of spoken language; **4F** use visual/contextual/peer/teacher support to read/comprehend texts

Comprehension

Read Together

 **TARGET SKILL** Compare and Contrast

Remember that when you **compare**, you tell how things are alike. When you **contrast**, you tell how things are different. Good readers compare and contrast things like characters, settings, or events as they read. How are markers and a paintbrush alike? How are they different?

markers

paintbrush

As you read **The Dot**, talk about how drawing and painting are the same and different. Write your ideas on a Venn diagram.

Drawing   Both   Painting

JOURNEYS DIGITAL Powered by DESTINATIONReading®
Comprehension Activities: Lesson 26

Read Together

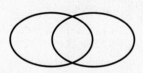

✔ **WORDS TO KNOW**

teacher	bear
studied	above
surprised	even
toward	pushed

✔ **TARGET SKILL**

Compare and Contrast
Tell how two things are alike or different.

✔ **TARGET STRATEGY**

Monitor/Clarify Read carefully. If a part doesn't make sense, reread it aloud correctly and then to yourself.

GENRE
Realistic fiction is a story that could happen in real life.

TEKS 1.4B ask questions/seek clarification/ locate details about texts; **1.4C** establish purpose/monitor comprehension; **RC-1(C)** monitor/adjust comprehension; **ELPS 4D** use prereading supports to comprehend texts

Meet the Author and Illustrator

Peter H. Reynolds

It took Peter H. Reynolds a year and a half to write **The Dot**. He named his character Vashti after a young girl he met at a coffee shop. Mr. Reynolds wrote **Ish** as a follow-up book to **The Dot**.

the dot

by Peter H. Reynolds

Art class was over, but Vashti sat
glued to her chair.

Her paper was empty.

Vashti's teacher leaned over the blank paper.
"Ah! A polar bear in a snow storm," she said.
"Very funny!" said Vashti. "I just CAN'T draw!"

Her teacher smiled.

"Just make a mark and
see where it takes you."

Vashti grabbed a marker and
gave the paper a good, strong jab.

"There!"

Her teacher picked up the paper
and studied it carefully.

"Hmmmmm."

She pushed the paper toward
Vashti and quietly said,
"Now sign it."

Vashti thought for a moment.

"Well, maybe I can't draw,
but I CAN sign my name."

The next week,
when Vashti walked into art class,
she was surprised to see what was
hanging above her teacher's desk.

It was the little dot
she had drawn—HER DOT!
All framed in swirly gold!

✔ STOP AND THINK

Compare and Contrast
Does Vashti have a different
feeling about her dot now?
Explain.

TEKS 1.9B, 1.14B, ELPS 4I

"Hmmph!
I can make a better dot than THAT!"

She opened her
never-before-used set of
watercolors and set to work.

Vashti painted and painted.
A red dot. A purple dot.
A yellow dot. A blue dot.

The blue mixed with the yellow.
She discovered that she could make
a GREEN dot.

Vashti kept experimenting.
Lots of little dots in many colors.

"If I can make little dots,
I can make BIG dots, too."

Vashti splashed her colors with
a bigger brush on bigger paper
to make bigger dots.

Vashti even made a dot
by NOT painting a dot.

At the school art show a few weeks later,
Vashti's many dots made quite a splash.

Vashti noticed a little boy gazing up at her.

"You're a really great artist.
I wish I could draw," he said.

"I bet you can," said Vashti.

"ME? No, not me. I can't draw
a straight line with a ruler."

Vashti smiled.

She handed the boy
a blank sheet of paper.
"Show me."

The boy's pencil shook
as he drew his line.

Vashti stared at the boy's squiggle.
And then she said . . .

"Sign it."

1. What is a <u>teacher</u>?

   ⬭ A person who lives at school

   ⬭ A person who gives art shows

   ⬭ A person who helps you learn

   TEKS 1.6C

2. ✔ TARGET SKILL **Compare and Contrast**

   How is Vashti's artwork at the beginning of the story different from her artwork at the end? How is it the same? **TEKS** 1.4B, 1.9B

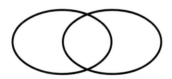

3. **Oral Language** Act out the story as though you are Vashti's teacher. Use the Retelling Cards.

   TEKS 1.9A, RC–1(E); **ELPS** 4G

Retelling Cards

TEKS **1.4B** ask questions/seek clarification/locate details about texts; **1.6C** use syntax/context to determine meaning; **1.9A** retell story events; **1.9B** describe/analyze characters; **RC–1(E)** retell/act out important story events; **ELPS 4G** demonstrate comprehension through shared reading/retelling/responding/note-taking

Henry and Dad Go Camping

by Ting Biderman

illustrated by Stacey Schuett

Dad put up the tent. Henry hurried to pump up the beds. Dad was sleepy, but Henry gazed up at the stars.

Then Henry sat up surprised.
What was that hissing sound?
Henry poked his dad and woke
him up.

"What's hissing?" Dad asked.

"It's creepy," said Henry. "It must be snakes!"

"Snakes?" asked Dad. "Maybe."

Dad shined a light toward the grass.
"I can see something that's long and
thin like a snake," Dad said.
"Is it hissing?" asked Henry.

"No," Dad said. "It's not hissing.
It's just a rope."

"The hissing hasn't stopped! What
can it be?" Henry asked.

Dad flashed the light inside the tent.
"Look at your bed, Henry," said Dad.
"It's getting as flat as a pancake. Your
leaky bed is hissing, not snakes."

Henry felt silly but safe. He felt
sleepy, too. He went to sleep as his
flat bed hissed its last hiss.

Artists Create Art!

Connect to Social Studies

✓ **WORDS TO KNOW**

teacher · bear
studied · above
surprised · even
toward · pushed

GENRE

A **biography** tells about events in a person's life. Find facts about artists' lives in this article.

TEXT FOCUS

Captions tell more information about a photo or picture. Use the captions and photos to find out more about pieces of art.

TEKS **1.3H** identify/read high-frequency words; **1.14B** identify important facts/details; **1.14D** use text features to locate information; **ELPS** **4I** employ reading skills to demonstrate comprehension

Artists Create Art!

by Anne Rogers

An artist makes art. Some artists paint pictures. Other artists make things.

David Wynne made this grizzly bear. It stands above a pond in New York.

David Wynne's sculpture "Grizzly Bear" is at the Donald M. Kendall Sculpture Gardens.

Seated Figures, Study for "A Sunday Afternoon on the Island of the Grande Jatte" by Georges Seurat

Georges Seurat went to art school in France. Look at his painting. Once you have studied it, you will see it is made of many brushstrokes. Are you surprised?

Tressa "Grandma" Prisbrey used glass bottles to make her art. She learned by herself. No teacher helped her.

Grandma Prisbrey made the wishing well shown below. She even made a building where her grandchildren played.

wishing well

Now turn toward a window. Think about what would happen if you pushed your paintbrush across the sky. What would your picture be?

Making Connections

Read Together

 Text to Self

TEKS 1.27A, 1.28, 1.29, RC-1(F)

Talk About Feelings How do you feel when you try your best? Compare and share ideas with a partner.

Text to Text

TEKS 1.24A, RC-1(F)

Connect to Art How are the paintings in the selections alike? Draw dots to make your own picture. Give it a title.

 Text to World

TEKS RC-1(F)

Make a List Make a list of ways that an artist can use his or her artwork.

 TEKS **1.24A** gather evidence; **1.27A** listen attentively/ask relevant questions; **1.28** share information/ideas by speaking clearly; **1.29** follow discussion rules; **RC-1(F)** make connections to experiences/texts/community; **ELPS** **1E** internalize new basic/academic language; **2I** demonstrate listening comprehension of spoken English; **3G** express opinions/ideas/feelings; **3J** respond orally to information in media

Grammar

Read Together

Exclamations A sentence that shows a strong feeling is called an **exclamation**. An exclamation begins with a capital letter and ends with an exclamation point.

You are a great artist**!**

That is such a beautiful painting**!**

Art class is so much fun**!**

46

Write each exclamation correctly.
Use another sheet of paper.

1. i can't wait for our school art show

2. this will be the best show ever

3. we are going to have a great time

4. ramon made such a tiny drawing

5. it is my very favorite in the show

Grammar in Writing

When you revise your writing, try using
some exclamations.

TEKS **1.17C** revise drafts; **1.19A** write brief compositions; **1.21C** recognize/use ending punctuation; **ELPS 5G** narrate/describe/explain in writing

Write to Respond

✔ **Voice** When you write **opinion sentences**, you can help readers hear your voice. Use exclamations to show your strong feelings.

Jill wrote an opinion about Vashti. Then she changed a sentence to an exclamation.

Revised Draft

really great !

I think Vashti is a ~~good~~ artist.

Writing Traits Checklist

✔ **Voice** Did I use exclamations to show my strong feelings?

✔ Are there any sentences that do not help explain my opinion? Did I delete them?

✔ Did I use the correct end marks?

48

In Jill's Final Copy, how does she show that she feels strongly about her opinion? Now edit your writing. Use the Checklist.

Final Copy

A Great Artist

I think Vashti is a really great artist!

One reason is she thinks of lots of ways to paint dots.

Another reason is that her paintings are very colorful.

Lesson 27

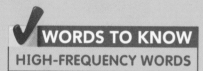

✓ WORDS TO KNOW
HIGH-FREQUENCY WORDS

different

near

enough

stories

high

always

once

happy

Vocabulary Reader

Context Cards

TEKS **1.3H** identify/read high-frequency words; **ELPS** **1F** use accessible language to learn new language; **3B** expand/internalize initial English vocabulary

Words to Know

Read Together

- Read each Context Card.

- Make up a new sentence that uses a blue word.

1 different
Children like to help out in different ways.

2 near
The girl helps plant flowers near the porch.

3 enough
Is there enough paint for everyone?

4 stories
They read silly stories to each other.

5 high
The girl helped him swing high!

6 always
She always helps her brother tie his shoes.

7 once
The boys cleaned up once they were done.

8 happy
She was happy to help wash the dog.

Background

✔ WORDS TO KNOW **Having Fun** What are some different ways to have fun? You can ride a bike near your home. You can swing high in the air. You can make up funny stories. Always take enough time to learn and have fun! Once you do, you will feel happy.

Ways to Have Fun

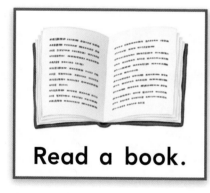

Read a book.

Ride a bike.

Swing high.

Kick a ball.

Tap a drum.

Name some ways you have fun.

TEKS 1.4C establish purpose/monitor comprehension; 1.14D use text features to locate information; 1.16A recognize media purposes; RC-1(A) establish reading purposes; ELPS 1E internalize new basic/academic language; 4F use visual/contextual/peer/teacher support to read/comprehend texts

Comprehension

Read Together

✓ **TARGET SKILL** Text and Graphic Features

When authors write about real things, they may use special text and features. **Special text** can be titles, labels, or captions. **Features** can be photos, graphs, maps, or drawings. Good readers use special text and features to get more information.

Colors We Like

United States

Dog

Graph   **Map**   **Drawing**

As you read **What Can You Do?**, notice the text and photos. Tell why they are used.

Feature	Purpose

WORDS TO KNOW

different	high
near	always
enough	once
stories	happy

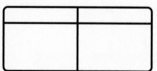

TARGET SKILL

Text and Graphic Features Tell how words go with photos.

TARGET STRATEGY

Analyze/Evaluate Tell how you feel about the text, and why.

GENRE

Informational text gives facts about a topic.

TEKS **1.3H** identify/read high-frequency words; **1.14D** use text features to locate information; **ELPS** **4D** use prereading supports to comprehend texts

Meet the Author and Photographer

Shelley Rotner

Shelley Rotner is both an author and an award-winning photographer. She has taken photographs of children from around the world.

Meet the Author

Sheila M. Kelly

What a team! Together, Sheila M. Kelly and Shelley Rotner have written about moms, dads, and grandparents. In this book, the two authors show that everyone has talents.

WHAT CAN YOU DO?

A BOOK ABOUT DISCOVERING WHAT YOU DO WELL

BY SHELLEY ROTNER AND SHEILA KELLY, ED.D.

PHOTOGRAPHS BY SHELLEY ROTNER

Essential Question

How do words and photos together give information?

55

"I know a boy
who can draw very
well and a girl who can
climb very high."

"We are all good at doing something.
We're always learning new things
as we get older."

"I like to swim
and learned how to float.
I had to practice.
Once I learned, I
felt like I could float for hours!"

"My little brother
is better on skis.
He can ski much faster
than I can."

We're happy when we
do something well,
whatever that might be.

"Reading is easy for me,
but math is much harder.
I'd like to be better at math, though."

✔ STOP AND THINK

Text and Graphic Features
Why does the author show
these two pictures together?

TEKS 1.14D; ELPS 4J

"I can't read very well yet.
I wish I could."

It can take a long time
to be good at something.
If we practice, things get
easier and easier to do.

Marie knows how to spell, and Jill prints well. Gene is really good at anything that has to do with computers.

"I haven't
discovered what
I'm good at yet."

Nathan writes funny stories about science.
Some of the funniest ones are
about a baby robot!
Beth likes to build.
The biggest tower she ever built
was taller than she is!

"I made the soccer team this year.
I hope I play well enough to score a goal."
"I see lots of things in the park.
I look near and far.
Things look much closer
through my binoculars!"

We all like to do what we do best.
When things are hard,
we need help to learn.
We might say, "I don't get it."

We're good at different things.

"I feed the baby myself now. When she gets bigger, she will not need help."

"I can fix my brother's wagon. I'm younger than my brother, but I'm good at fixing things."

"I got my training wheels off earlier than I thought I would.
I felt very proud!"

"The kids made me captain of our team. That was one of the happiest days of my life."

We have schoolwork, acting, singing,
dancing, playing games, or sports!
We all have something we do well.

What can you do?

Read Together

Your Turn

1. In the story, the word <u>different</u> means —

   ⬭ very strange

   ⬭ not like something else

   ⬭ the same as something else

                      TEKS 1.3H, 1.6C

2. ✔ TARGET SKILL **Text and Graphic Features**
Why are the words in quotation marks on
page 56? **TEKS** 1.4B; 1.14D; 1.24C **ELPS** 4I

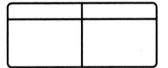

3. **Oral Language** Tell the main idea
of the selection. Use the Retelling
Cards to tell important facts
about the topic. **TEKS** 1.13, 1.14A, 1.14B, RC-1(E)

Retelling Cards

TEKS 1.3H identify/read high-frequency words; 1.4B ask questions/seek clarification/locate details about texts; 1.6C use syntax/context to determine meaning; 1.13 identify topic/explain author's purpose; 1.14A restate main idea; 1.14B identify important facts/details; 1.14D use text features to locate information; 1.24C record information in visual formats; RC-1(E) retell/act out important story events; ELPS 4I employ reading skills to demonstrate comprehension

I Read

The Fox and the Grapes

retold by Lindsey Parr
illustrated by Jeff Mack

✔ PHONICS SKILL

Endings **-er, -est**
Syllable **-le**

✔ WORDS TO KNOW

near
always
happy

TEKS **1.3C(i)** decode using closed syllables; **1.3C(iii)** decode using final stable syllables; **1.3E** read words with inflectional endings; **1.3H** identify/ read high-frequency words; **ELPS** **4A** learn English sound-letter relationships/decode

The Fox and the Grapes

retold by Lindsey Pare
illustrated by Jeff Mack

Digger Fox is always happy to see Gram. Gram has a big back porch. Digger is happiest there. Grapes grow near that porch.

Gram brings lunch. She brings the reddest apples Digger has ever seen. He likes grapes better, but the grapes aren't ripe yet.

Gram goes inside. Digger has a plan. He jiggles the benches closer to the grapes. He just has to have a grape!

Digger jiggles himself up. He reaches for the biggest bunch of grapes. He wiggles up, up, up. Then Digger tumbles down. Gram catches him.

Gram cuddles Digger and tells him,
"You must be the luckiest little fox ever.
I got here just in time."

"Can't I eat one grape, Gram?" asks
Digger.

Gram reaches for a grape and hands it to Digger. He tastes it.

"Yuck," he grumbles. "It tastes like a pickle!"

"Yes," winks Gram. "The grapes aren't ripe yet. Next time, trust me."

Digger puts the benches back in place. Gram will ask Digger back when the grapes get ripe. Digger can't wait! Those grapes are much tastier when they are ripe!

Connect to Traditional Tales

✓ **WORDS TO KNOW**

different	high
near	always
enough	once
stories	happy

GENRE

A **fable** is a short story in which a character learns a lesson.

TEXT FOCUS

A **moral** of a fable is the lesson that a character learns. What lesson do you learn from this fable?

TEKS **1.3E** read words with inflectional endings; **1.3H** identify/read high-frequency words; **1.7A** connect stories/fables with personal experiences

Readers' Theater

The Wind and the Sun

an Aesop's fable

Cast

Narrator

Wind

Sun

Traveler

Narrator Sometimes stories teach a lesson. In this story, Wind and Sun have different ideas about who is stronger.

Wind I am stronger.

Sun No, I am stronger.

Wind That's enough bragging. Let's have a contest. I know **I** will win.

Sun I'll be happy to have a contest.

Wind Okay. I see a traveler coming near. Whoever gets the traveler to take off that coat is stronger.

Narrator First Wind began to blow very hard. Once Wind started, it did not stop.

Traveler That wind is always so cold. I need to wrap my coat tight around me.

83

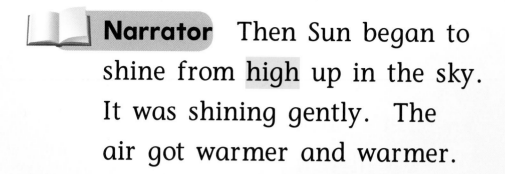

Narrator Then Sun began to shine from high up in the sky. It was shining gently. The air got warmer and warmer.

Traveler Now it's nice and warm. I can take off my heavy coat.

Narrator The moral is: "It is better to use kindness instead of force."

Making Connections

Read Together

Text to Self TEKS 1.19A, RC-1(F)

Write About Yourself

Write sentences that tell what you do best.

Text to Text TEKS 1.29, RC-1(F)

Talk About It In a group, decide what Wind and Sun should do if they want the traveler to put his coat back on.

 Text to World TEKS 1.19A, RC-1(F)

Connect to Social Studies Think of a person you know who tries hard. Write about how that person does his or her best.

 TEKS **1.19A** write brief compositions; **1.29** follow discussion rules; **RC-1(F)** make connections to experiences/texts/community; **ELPS 1E** internalize new basic/academic language; **5B** write using new basic/content-based vocabulary; **5G** narrate/describe/explain in writing

Grammar

Kinds of Sentences Different kinds of sentences have different jobs. Every sentence begins with a capital letter and ends with an end mark.

A **statement** tells something.
She is in a play.

A **question** asks something.
Would you like to be
in plays?

An **exclamation** shows a strong feeling.
I love acting in plays!

Write each sentence correctly.
Use another sheet of paper.

1. Emma can climb high

2. did Jamal learn to ski

3. She is a great dancer?

4. my friend builds things

5. What can you do.

Grammar in Writing

When you revise your writing, try using
some different kinds of sentences.

TEKS **1.17D** edit drafts; **1.19A** write brief compositions; **1.22E** use resources to find correct spellings; **ELPS 5C** spell English words with increasing accuracy; **5F** use a variety of sentence types in writing; **5G** narrate/describe/explain in writing

Write to Respond (Read Together)

✓ **Sentence Fluency** Good **opinion sentences** give reasons. Sometimes you can explain a reason by using the word **because**.

Raul wrote an opinion about skiing. Then he added words to explain his first reason.

Revised Draft

because you can go fast
It is exciting.
^

 **Writing Traits Checklist**

✓ **Sentence Fluency** Did I use the word **because** to explain one reason?

✓ Does my topic sentence tell my opinion?

✓ Do my sentences end with the correct mark?

✓ Did I check my spelling with a dictionary?

What words does Raul use to explain why skiing is exciting? Use the Checklist to revise your sentences.

Final Copy

Fun on Skis

Skiing is so much fun!

It is exciting because you can go fast.

I also like jumping over big piles of snow.

second

ball

across

head

heard

large

cried

should

Vocabulary Reader	Context Cards

TEKS 1.3H identify/read high-frequency words; **ELPS** 1F use accessible language to learn new language; 3B expand/internalize initial English vocabulary

Words to Know

Read Together

● Read each Context Card.

● Ask a question that uses one of the blue words.

1

second

The boy is trying to tie his second sneaker.

2

ball

She practiced until she could hit the ball well.

3 across

The runners dashed across the finish line.

4 head

He hit the ball with his head to make a goal.

5 heard

The children heard clapping at the end.

6 large

It was not too hard to ride up the large hill.

7 cried

"We can do it!" cried the team.

8 should

The teacher said that she should try again.

Background (Read Together)

✓ **WORDS TO KNOW** **Flying a Kite** Have you heard that flying a kite is fun? You should try it on a breezy day. Get a kite and a large ball of string. Hold the kite above your head. Run across the grass. If that doesn't work, try a second time. Soon you will have cried, "The kite is flying!"

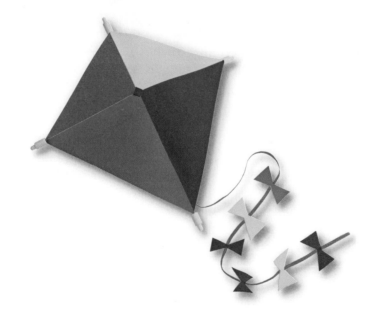

- What does cried mean in the sentence?
- Did you ever fly a kite? Tell about it.
- Would you like to fly one? Why or why not?

TEKS 1.4C establish purpose/monitor comprehension; **1.9A** retell story events; **1.9B** describe/analyze characters; **RC-1(A)** establish reading purposes; **ELPS** **1E** internalize new basic/academic language; **4F** use visual/contextual/peer/teacher support to read/comprehend texts

Comprehension

Read Together

✓ **TARGET SKILL** Story Structure   A story has different parts. The **characters** are the people and animals in a story. The **setting** is when and where a story takes place. The **plot** is the order of story events. The plot tells about a problem the characters have and what they do to solve it.

What problem does this character have?

As you read **The Kite**, think about Frog and Toad's problem and how it is solved.

Characters	Setting
Plot	

JOURNEYS DIGITAL Powered by DESTINATIONReading®
Comprehension Activities: Lesson 28

✔ **WORDS TO KNOW**

second	heard
ball	large
across	cried
head	should

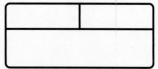

✔ **TARGET SKILL**

Story Structure Tell the setting, characters, and events in a story.

✔ **TARGET STRATEGY**

Infer/Predict Use clues to figure out more about story parts.

GENRE

A **fantasy** story could not happen in real life.

TEKS **1.3H** identify/read high-frequency words; **1.4B** ask questions/seek clarification/locate details about texts; **RC-1(D)** make inferences/use textual evidence; **ELPS 4D** use prereading supports to comprehend texts

Meet the Author and Illustrator

Arnold Lobel

Arnold Lobel drew many animals before he came up with the frog and toad characters. During vacations with his family in Vermont, Mr. Lobel watched his children play with frogs and toads. Soon the animals were starring in his books.

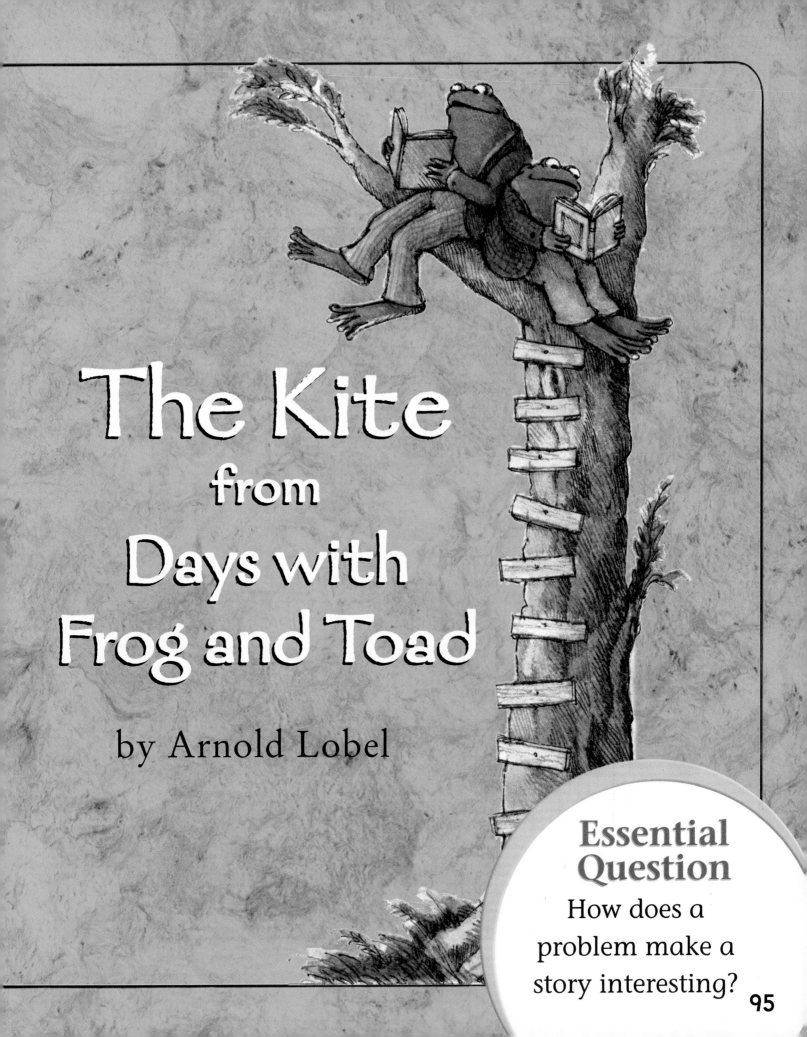

The Kite
from
Days with Frog and Toad

by Arnold Lobel

Essential Question

How does a problem make a story interesting?

95

The Kite

Frog and Toad went out
to fly a kite.
They went to a large meadow
where the wind was strong.
"Our kite will fly up and up,"
said Frog.
"It will fly all the way up
to the top of the sky."
"Toad," said Frog,
"I will hold the ball of string.
You hold the kite and run."

Toad ran across the meadow.
He ran as fast as his short legs
could carry him.
The kite went up in the air.
It fell to the ground with a bump.
Toad heard laughter.
Three robins were sitting in a bush.

"That kite will not fly,"
said the robins.
"You may as well give up."

Toad ran back to Frog.
"Frog," said Toad,
"this kite will not fly. I give up."

 **STOP AND THINK**

Story Structure What problem
do Frog and Toad have?

TEKS 1.9A, **ELPS** 4I

"We must make a second try," said
Frog. "Wave the kite over your head.
Perhaps that will make it fly."

Toad ran back across the meadow.
He waved the kite over his head.

The kite went up in the air
and then fell down with a thud.
"What a joke!" said the robins.
"That kite will never
get off the ground."

Toad ran back to Frog.

"This kite is a joke," he said.

"It will never get off the ground."

"We have to make
a third try," said Frog.

"Wave the kite over your head
and jump up and down.

Perhaps that will make it fly."

Toad ran across the meadow again.
He waved the kite over his head.
He jumped up and down.
The kite went up in the air and
crashed down into the grass.

"That kite is junk," said the robins.
"Throw it away and go home."
Toad ran back to Frog.
"This kite is junk," he said.
"I think we should throw
it away and go home."

"Toad," said Frog,
"we need one more try.
Wave the kite over your head.
Jump up and down
and shout UP KITE UP."

Toad ran across the meadow.
He waved the kite over his head.
He jumped up and down.
He shouted, "UP KITE UP!"

The kite flew into the air.
It climbed higher and higher.
"We did it!" cried Toad.

"Yes," said Frog.
"If a running try
did not work,
a running and waving try
did not work,
and a running, waving,
and jumping try
did not work,
I knew that
a running, waving, jumping,
and shouting try
just had to work."

The robins flew out of the bush.
But they could not fly
as high as the kite.
Frog and Toad sat
and watched their kite.
It seemed to be flying
way up at the top of the sky.

Read Together **Your Turn**

1. In the story, the word <u>large</u> means —

⬭ very big

⬭ very small

⬭ very high

TEKS 1.3H, 1.6C

2. ✓ TARGET SKILL **Story Structure**

How do Frog and Toad solve their problem?
TEKS 1.4B, 1.9A

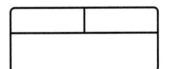

3. Oral Language Act out the story. Decide who will be Frog, Toad, and the robins. Use the Retelling Cards to help you. TEKS 1.9A, RC-1(E); ELPS 4G

Retelling Cards

 TEKS 1.3H identify/read high-frequency words; **1.4B** ask questions/seek clarification/locate details about texts; **1.6C** use syntax/context to determine meaning; **1.9A** retell story events; **RC–1(E)** retell/act out important story events; **ELPS 4G** demonstrate comprehension through shared reading/retelling/responding/note-taking

Bird
Watching

by Rebecca McDermott

This is a large bird. Three large eggs can fit in its nest. That huge nest is quite a sight!

This bird has a long bill. It flies low across the sea. It scoops up a lot of fish in that long bill!

Look at this bird's long, bright tail! It looks like a fan. Its tail is shiniest in sunlight. This bird is fun to see.

This hawk can take flight high across the sky. Then it can dive down in a flash. It can fly faster than a racecar can race!

Which bird is the fastest
swimmer? Few birds swim, but this
one can zoom right by. It looks like
it is flying in water!

This bird is the biggest and
the strongest. One of its eggs is
as big as 24 hen's eggs. It is the
fastest runner, too!

What can this bird do best?
It sings the sweetest songs. Hush.
You might hear it!

Connect to Science

GENRE

Informational text gives facts about a topic. Find facts about weather in this article.

TEXT FOCUS

A **graph** is a drawing that uses numbers, pictures, or symbols to give information. What does the graph on p. 120 show?

TEKS 1.3H identify/read high-frequency words; 1.14B identify important facts/details; 1.14D use text features to locate information

Measuring Weather

There are different tools for measuring weather.

Have you ever heard of a windsock? It shows which way the wind blows.

A rain gauge measures how much rain falls. A large storm will bring a lot of rain.

A thermometer measures temperature. Temperature is how warm or cool something is.

On a hot day, your friends might have cried, "Let's ride bikes and play ball!"

On a cold day, your mother might have said, "You should wear a hat on your head."

When you know the temperature, you know what to wear.

Look at the bars across the graph.
Each bar shows the temperature for a day.
Which day was the hottest? Which day
was the coolest? What was the temperature
on the second day of the week?

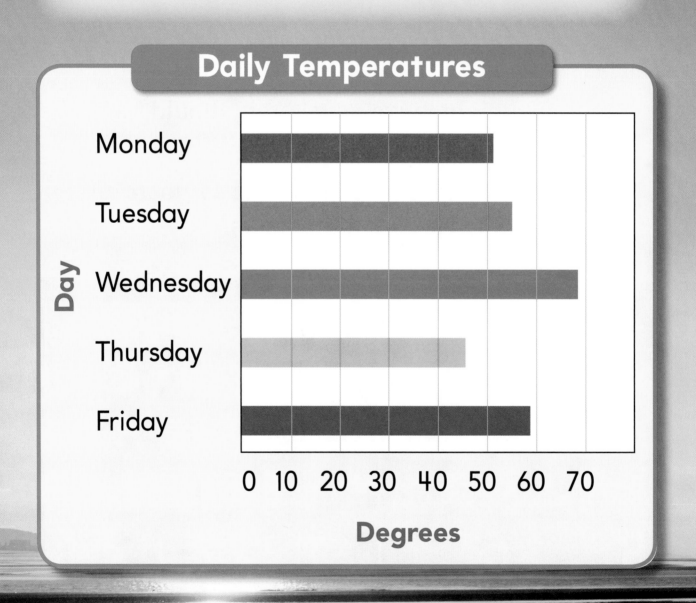

Daily Temperatures

Day

Monday
Tuesday
Wednesday
Thursday
Friday

0 10 20 30 40 50 60 70

Degrees

Making Connections

 Text to Self   TEKS 1.7A, 1.28

Share Think about the fun Frog and Toad had on the windy day. Tell a partner what you do on windy days.

 Text to Text   TEKS 1.11, 1.19C, RC-1(F)

Write to Describe What was the weather like when Frog and Toad flew a kite? Write about it. Use words that tell how things looked, moved, and sounded.

 Text to World   TEKS 1.4B, RC-1(F)

Connect to Science Read nonfiction books to find facts about weather. Read carefully and look at the pictures to help you figure out information. Write two facts.

 TEKS **1.4B** ask questions/seek clarification/locate details about texts; **1.7A** connect stories/fables to personal experiences; **1.11** recognize sensory details; **1.19C** write brief comments on text; **1.28** share information/ideas by speaking clearly; **RC-1(F)** make connections to experiences/texts/community; **ELPS** **3H** narrate/describe/explain with detail; **5B** write using new basic/content-based vocabulary

TEKS **1.11** recognize sensory details; **1.17C** revise drafts; **1.17D** edit drafts; **1.20A(iii)** understand/use adjectives; **ELPS** **1E** internalize new basic/academic language; **5D** edit writing for standard grammar/usage; **5E** employ increasingly complex grammatical structures in writing

Grammar

Kinds of Adjectives Some adjectives describe by telling how things **taste, smell, sound,** or **feel.**

Taste	We ate sweet berries before we flew kites.
Smell	The air smelled fresh and clean.
Sound	We gave a loud cheer when our kites flew up!
Feel	The warm sun shined down on us.

Work with a partner. Find the adjective in each sentence. Decide if it tells how something tastes, smells, sounds, or feels. Then use the adjective in a new sentence.

1. Sam shared his sour pickles at our picnic.

2. Our kites flew in the cool breeze.

3. Some crickets made noisy chirps.

4. We ate some salty chips.

5. Our pie smelled delicious!

Grammar in Writing

When you revise your writing, look for places to add adjectives to tell how things taste, smell, sound, or feel.

Write to Respond

Read Together

☑ **Word Choice** When you write **opinion sentences**, don't use the same words again and again. Use different words to tell more.

Matt wrote about the robins. Later, he changed words to make his ideas clearer.

Revised Draft

The three robins were mean.
~~laughed at Frog and Toad.~~
They ~~did mean things.~~
^

Writing Traits Checklist

☑ **Word Choice** Did I add adjectives and other exact words to make my ideas clear?

☑ Did I write reasons that explain my opinion?

☑ Did I use a dictionary, Glossary, or word list to check my spelling?

124

Which words in Matt's final copy explain how the robins were mean? Now revise your writing. Use the Checklist.

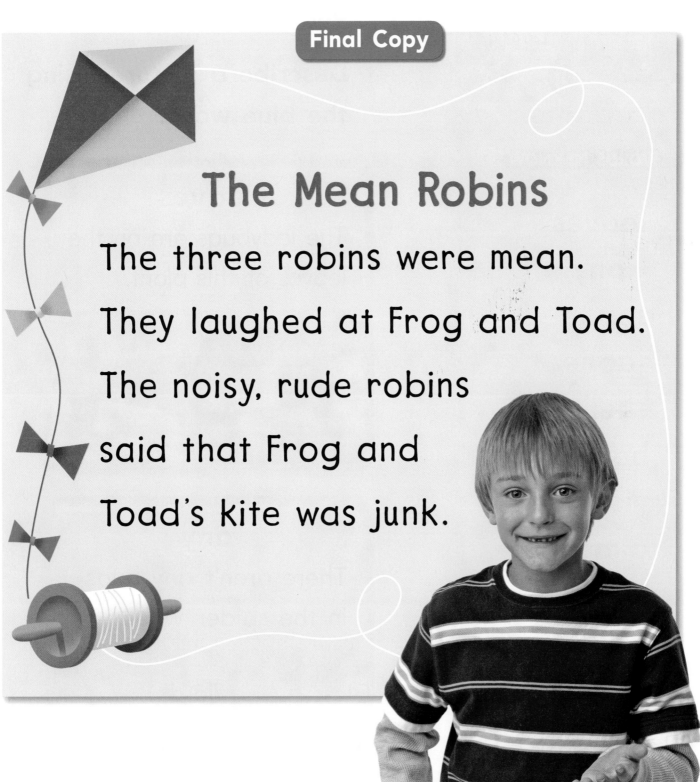

Final Copy

The Mean Robins

The three robins were mean.

They laughed at Frog and Toad.

The noisy, rude robins

said that Frog and

Toad's kite was junk.

✔ **WORDS TO KNOW**
HIGH-FREQUENCY WORDS

leaves

any

happened

gone

hello

behind

idea

almost

Vocabulary Reader

Context Cards

TEKS **1.3H** identify/read high-frequency words; **ELPS** **1F** use accessible language to learn new language; **3B** expand/internalize initial English vocabulary

Words to Know

Read Together

● **Read each Context Card.**

● **Describe a picture, using the blue word.**

1

leaves

The ladybugs are on the leaves of this plant.

2

any

There aren't any bugs in the spider web.

3 happened

What happened to the wasps' nest?

4 gone

The moths are gone, but they left eggs.

5 hello

The bees seem to say hello to each other.

6 behind

Do you see the grass behind the ant hill?

7 idea

Here is an idea, or plan, for a project.

8 almost

This bug has almost finished eating.

Background

✔ **WORDS TO KNOW**   **How Insects Move**

To learn how insects move, here's an idea. Say hello loudly. Almost any insect will move. An ant will crawl away. A ladybug will fly from the leaves. A grasshopper will hop fast behind tall grass. Write about what happened before the insects are gone.

Insects

grasshopper

ant

ladybug

bumblebee

What does leaves mean in the sentence?
Name some more insects.

TEKS **1.4C** establish purpose/monitor comprehension; **RC-1(A)** establish reading purposes; **RC-1(D)** make inferences/use textual evidence; **ELPS 1E** internalize new basic/academic language; **4F** use visual/contextual/peer/teacher support to read/comprehend texts

Comprehension

Read Together

✓ **TARGET SKILL** Cause and Effect

Remember that one story event can lead
to another. The **cause** is the reason why
something happens. The **effect**
is what happens. Good readers
think about cause and effect to
better understand what happens
in a story and why it happens.

Cause: The boy played ball inside.
What is the **effect**?

As you read **A Boat Disappears**, think
about what Skeet does to find his boat.

What happens?	Why?

✔ **WORDS TO KNOW**

leaves	hello
any	behind
happened	idea
gone	almost

✔ **TARGET SKILL**

Cause and Effect Tell what happens and why.

✔ **TARGET STRATEGY**

Visualize Picture what is happening as you read.

GENRE

A **mystery** is a story about a character who solves a puzzle.

TEKS **1.3H** identify/read high-frequency words; **1.9A** retell story events; **RC-1(C)** monitor/adjust comprehension; **ELPS** **4D** use prereading supports to comprehend texts

Meet the Author and Illustrator

Doug Cushman

Doug Cushman says, "A good character will almost write a book by himself." Some of his characters include Aunt Eater, a mystery-solving anteater, and Nick Trunk, an elephant detective. In this story, you will meet Inspector Hopper and McBugg.

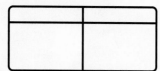

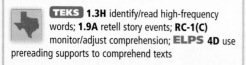

A Boat Disappears

from **Inspector Hopper**

by Doug Cushman

Essential Question

How do some story events make other events happen?

Solving a mystery can be tricky. You may
look behind and beneath things for clues.
You are almost sure to solve it if
you go to a helpful detective,
like the one in this story.

A Boat Disappears

Skeet walked into the office
of Inspector Hopper.
"My boat disappeared," he said.
"That *is* a mystery,"
said Inspector Hopper.
"Tell us what happened."

"I sailed my boat this morning,"
said Skeet.
"Then I went to lunch.
When I came back after lunch,
my boat was gone!"

"What did your boat look like?"
asked Inspector Hopper.
"Here is a picture," said Skeet.
"It looks like a leaf," said McBugg.
"It *is* a leaf," said Skeet,
"but it is a good boat."

"We will take your case,"
said Inspector Hopper.
"Show us where your boat was
the last time you saw it.
Let's go, McBugg!"

✔ STOP AND THINK
Cause and Effect
Why did Skeet go to
see Inspector Hopper?

TEKS 1.9B, ELPS 4J

They all went to the lake.
"Here is where my boat was,"
said Skeet.

"Hmm," said Inspector Hopper.
"I don't see any footprints.
But wait! What is this?"

"It looks like a piece of my boat,"
said Skeet.
"Here is another piece,"
said Inspector Hopper.
"Let's follow this trail."

They followed the trail of boat pieces.
The trail went past a water spout.
"Hello, Eensy Weensy,"
said Inspector Hopper.
"We are looking for a missing boat."
"What does it look like?"
asked Eensy Weensy.
"Here is a picture," said Skeet.
"It looks like a leaf,"
said Eensy Weensy.
"It *is* a leaf," said Skeet,
"but it is a good boat."

"I have not seen your boat,"
said Eensy Weensy.
"I'm trying to get back up
this water spout.
The rain washed me out."
"Thank you anyway,"
said Inspector Hopper.

Inspector Hopper, McBugg, and Skeet
followed the trail.
"Hello, Sally," said Inspector Hopper.
"We are looking for a missing boat.
Here is a picture of it."
"It looks like a leaf," said Sally.
"It *is* a leaf," said Skeet,
"but it is a good boat."

"I have not seen it," said Sally.
"I have been jogging all morning.
I have already jogged three feet."
"Thank you anyway,"
said Inspector Hopper.
Inspector Hopper, McBugg, and Skeet
followed the trail.

"Hello, Conrad," said Inspector Hopper.
"We are looking for a missing boat.
Here is a picture of it."
"I have seen it," said Conrad.
"Hooray!" said Skeet.
"Where is it?"

"I ate it," said Conrad.

"What?" said Skeet.

"You ate my boat?"

"Yes," said Conrad.

"It looked like a leaf.

So I ate it.

I did not know it was your boat."

"What will I do now?" asked Skeet.

Inspector Hopper looked around.
"There are many leaves here,"
he said.
"Perhaps Conrad can help you pick
out a new boat."
"I would be happy to help,"
said Conrad.
"Thank you," said Skeet.
"Maybe you can pick out a boat
that isn't so yummy."
"That is a good idea," said Conrad.

147

"Another mystery solved!"
said Inspector Hopper.
"I wonder what a boat tastes like?"
asked McBugg."
"Let's go home,"
said Inspector Hopper.

148

Read Together

Your Turn

1. In the story, the word <u>behind</u> means —

⬭ in back of

⬭ on top of

⬭ in front of

TEKS 1.3H, 1.6C

2. ✓ **TARGET SKILL** **Cause and Effect**

What happened when Conrad saw Skeet's boat? **TEKS** 1.4B, 1.9B, **ELPS** 4G

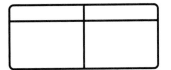

3. Oral Language Take turns telling the story with a partner. Use the Retelling Cards to help you.

TEKS 1.9A, RC–1(E)

Retelling Cards

 TEKS **1.3H** identify/read high-frequency words; **1.4B** ask questions/seek clarification/locate details about texts; **1.6C** use syntax/context to determine meaning; **1.9A** retell story events; **1.9B** describe/analyze characters; **RC–1(E)** retell/act out important story events; **ELPS 4G** demonstrate comprehension through shared reading/retelling/responding/note-taking

149

Ruth's Day

by Brady Frances
illustrated by Hideko Takahashi

150

Buzz! The clock buzzed loudly.
Ruth slowly got out of bed.

Ruth sat at the table and ate her
Crunchy Pops. She was still sleepy.

It was chilly, so Ruth got
dressed quickly. Her bus came
down the road slowly. Ruth was
almost late!

The bus stopped and beeped.
Ruth was just in time. She sat
behind the driver. Ruth had not
missed the bus. She felt happy.

Ruth sat with Edith. Edith smiled
sweetly. Ruth smiled back. It was fun
to sit with Edith. Ruth felt happy.

"Knock, knock," said Edith.

"I know that joke," said Ruth.
"It's funny."

"It's goofy," said Edith.

Ruth and Edith grinned. The bus went
on slowly. At last, it got to the school.

Ruth and Edith sat in class.
Edith had left her math book at
home. Ruth let Edith use hers.
Edith was grateful.

Edith smiled and said, "You're a
good pal, Ruth." Ruth felt happy.

When Ruth got home, Mom gave
her a big hug. Ruth felt so happy.
She had a great day!

Connect to Poetry

✓ **WORDS TO KNOW**

leaves	hello
any	behind
happened	idea
gone	almost

GENRE

Poetry uses the sound of words to show pictures and feelings. Which rhyming words make the poems fun to hear and say?

TEXT FOCUS

Rhythm is a pattern of beats, like music. Clap along with the rhythm of the poems.

TEKS **1.3H** identify/read high-frequency words; **1.8** respond to/use rhythm/rhyme/alliteration; **1.18B** write short poems; **ELPS** **4D** use prereading supports to comprehend texts

Busy Bugs

How do you think this poet got the idea to write a snail poem? Read how the snail says hello to the Sun.

Caracol, caracol

Caracol, caracol,
saca tus cuernos al sol.

To a Snail

Poke your head out, little one.
Time to say, "Good morning, Sun!"

traditional Spanish rhyme

Look for bugs behind rocks, on leaves, or in the grass. If a bug has wings, it may be gone before you know what happened.

Song of the Bugs

Some bugs pinch
And some bugs creep
Some bugs buzz themselves to sleep
Buzz Buzz Buzz Buzz
This is the song of the bugs.

Some bugs fly
When the moon is high
Some bugs make a light in the sky
Flicker, flicker firefly
This is the song of the bugs.

by Margaret Wise Brown

On almost any rainy day you will be sure to see worms. Watch them move!

Worm

Squiggly
Wiggly
Wriggly
Jiggly
Ziggly
Higgly
Piggly
Worm.

Watch it wiggle
Watch it wriggle
See it squiggle
See it squirm!

by Mary Ann Hoberman

Write About Bugs

Choose a bug you know about. Write a poem about it. Use rhyming words. Use words to tell what the bug looks like and how it moves.

Making Connections

 Read Together

 Text to Self TEKS 1.19A, RC-1(F)

Write a Caption Draw a picture of your favorite bug. Write a caption that tells how it moves.

 Text to Text TEKS RC-1(F)

Connect to Music Make up a bug song that Inspector Hopper might sing.

 Text to World TEKS 1.23B, RC-1(F)

Discuss Bugs Tell what kinds of bugs are in Texas. List books and other things to help you find out more about bugs.

 TEKS **1.19A** write brief compositions; **1.23B** determine relevant sources of information; **RC-1(F)** make connections to experiences/texts/community; **ELPS 1E** internalize new basic/academic language; **3J** respond orally to information in media; **5B** write using new basic/content-based vocabulary

Grammar

Adverbs   Adverbs are words that describe verbs. They can tell **how, where, when,** or **how much** something is. Many, but not all, adverbs end with <u>-ly</u>.

Adverbs	
How	The boat moves **quickly** in the water. They **carefully** steered the boat.
Where	They're **here**! The water splashed **everywhere**.
When	The bugs woke up **early** in the morning. They went to bed **late**.
How much	They kicked a ball **very** hard. The ball flew by **too** fast.

Turn and Talk

Work with a partner. Read each sentence and find the adverb. Decide if it tells how, where, when, or how much. Then say a new sentence, using the adverb.

1. Ned slowly unpacked the picnic basket.

2. His friends walk to get there.

3. Fred was very tired from the trip.

4. Bea cheerfully told a joke.

5. They want to have picnics often.

Grammar in Writing

When you revise your writing, look for places where you can add adverbs.

TEKS 1.17A generate ideas for writing; 1.17B develop drafts; **ELPS** 5B write using new basic/content-based vocabulary

Reading-Writing Workshop: Prewrite

Write to Respond

Read Together

 Ideas Before writing an **opinion paragraph**, list your opinion and reasons for that opinion. Think of examples to explain your reasons.

Tara wanted to write about Inspector Hopper. To help find good reasons and examples, she looked through the story again.

Explore a Topic

Prewrite Checklist

 Did I list my opinion?

 Did I give a few good reasons?

 Do my examples explain my reasons?

164

Read Tara's plan. What is her opinion? What are her reasons? Plan your opinion paragraph. Use the Checklist. Then write your draft.

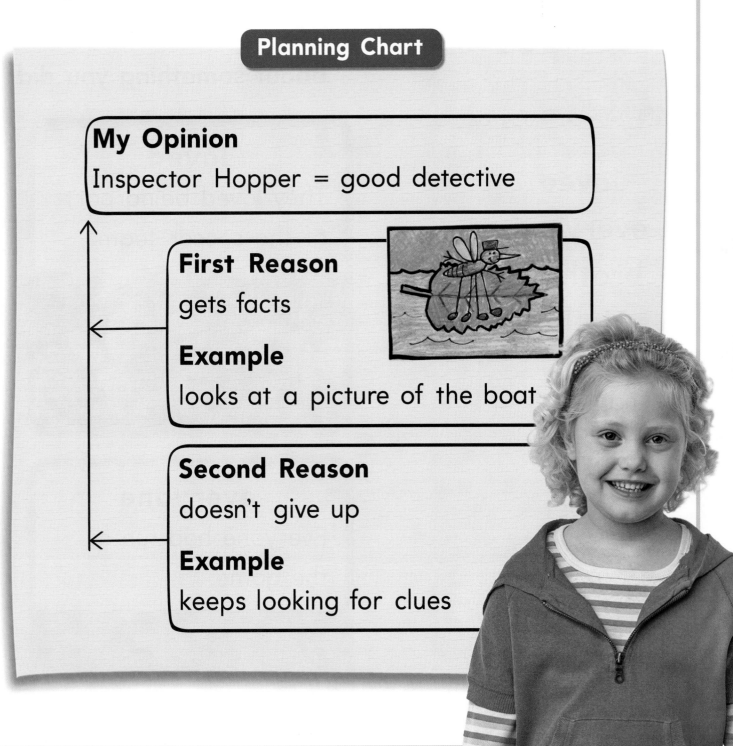

Planning Chart

My Opinion

Inspector Hopper = good detective

First Reason

gets facts

Example

looks at a picture of the boat

Second Reason

doesn't give up

Example

keeps looking for clues

WORDS TO KNOW

HIGH-FREQUENCY WORDS

loved

everyone

brothers

field

sorry

only

people

most

Vocabulary
Reader

Context
Cards

TEKS 1.3H identify/read high-frequency
words; **ELPS** 1F use accessible language to
learn new language; 3B expand/internalize initial
English vocabulary

Words
to Know

Read Together

- Read each Context Card.

- Use a blue word to tell about something you did.

1

loved

They loved being part of the soccer team.

2

everyone

Everyone had fun at the game.

3 brothers

The brothers are on the same team.

4 field

The field was wet after the rain.

5 sorry

The girl was sorry she couldn't play today.

6 only

The Reds are ahead by only one point.

7 people

People were happy after the game.

8 most

The team cheered most for their coach.

167

Background

✓ **WORDS TO KNOW** **Mia Hamm** Mia Hamm has never been sorry to be playing sports. Even when she was little, she loved soccer the most. She learned from her brothers and sisters. At only fifteen, Mia played on the United States soccer team. Many people watched Mia on the field. Everyone cheered!

Have you ever won anything?
What did it feel like to win?

TEKS 1.4C establish purpose/monitor comprehension; 1.9B describe/analyze characters; RC-1(A) establish reading purposes; ELPS 1E internalize new basic/academic language; 4F use visual/contextual/peer/teacher support to read/comprehend texts

Comprehension

Read Together

☑ **TARGET SKILL** Understanding Characters

Remember that **characters** are the people and animals in a story. You can learn about story characters from the things they say and do. Good readers use these clues to figure out how characters feel and why they do the things they do.

How do these characters feel? What clues helped you?

As you read **Winners Never Quit!**, think about what Mia says and how she acts.

Speaking	Acting	Feeling

JOURNEYS DIGITAL Powered by DESTINATIONReading
Comprehension Activities: Lesson 30

✔ **WORDS TO KNOW**

loved	sorry
everyone	only
brothers	people
field	most

✔ **TARGET SKILL**

Understanding Characters Tell more about characters.

✔ **TARGET STRATEGY**

Summarize Stop to tell important ideas as you read.

GENRE

Narrative nonfiction tells a true story.

TEKS 1.9B describe/analyze characters; 1.14B identify important facts/details; **RC-1(C)** monitor/adjust comprehension; **RC-1(D)** make inferences/use textual evidence; **ELPS** 4D use prereading supports to comprehend text

Meet the Author

Mia Hamm

Mia Hamm went from playing football to soccer at age fourteen. She became one of the best women's soccer players ever. She knows what it takes to be a good teammate!

Meet the Illustrator

Carol Thompson

Carol Thompson has won many awards for illustrating children's picture books. She also makes greeting cards. She lives in England with her family.

Winners Never Quit!

by Mia Hamm

illustrated by Carol Thompson

Essential Question

What can you learn from story characters?

171

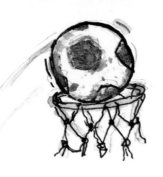

Mia loved basketball.

Mia loved baseball.

But most of all, Mia loved
soccer. She played every
day with her brothers
and sisters.

Tap, tap, tap. Her toes kept the ball right where she wanted it. Then, *smack*! She'd kick the ball straight into the net. **Goal!** Everyone on her team would cheer.

But sometimes it didn't work that way.
One day, no matter how hard she tried,
Mia couldn't score a goal.

The ball sailed to
the left of the net.

Or to the right.

Or her sister Lovdy,
the goalie, saved the
ball with her hands.

No goal.

No cheering.

"Too bad, Mia," her brother Garrett said. "Better luck next time!"

But Mia didn't want better luck next time. She wanted better luck *now*.

"I Quit!"

Mia said.

"You can't quit!" Lovdy said. Then we'll only have two people on our team."

"Come on, Mia," her sister Caroline pleaded. "You always quit when you start losing."

"Just keep playing, Mia," Garrett said. "It'll be fun."

But losing wasn't fun. Mia stomped
back to the house.

✔ STOP AND THINK

Understanding Characters
Why would Mia rather quit
than lose?

TEKS 1.9B, RC-1(D), ELPS 4K

"Quitter!"

"Quitter!" Lovdy yelled.
Mia didn't care.
She'd rather quit than lose.

The next day, Mia ran outside, ready to play soccer. When she got there, the game had already started.

"Hey!" she yelled. "Why didn't you wait for me?"

Garrett stopped playing.

"Sorry, Mia," he said. "But quitters can't play on my team."

"Yeah," said Lovdy. "If you can't learn to lose, you can't play."

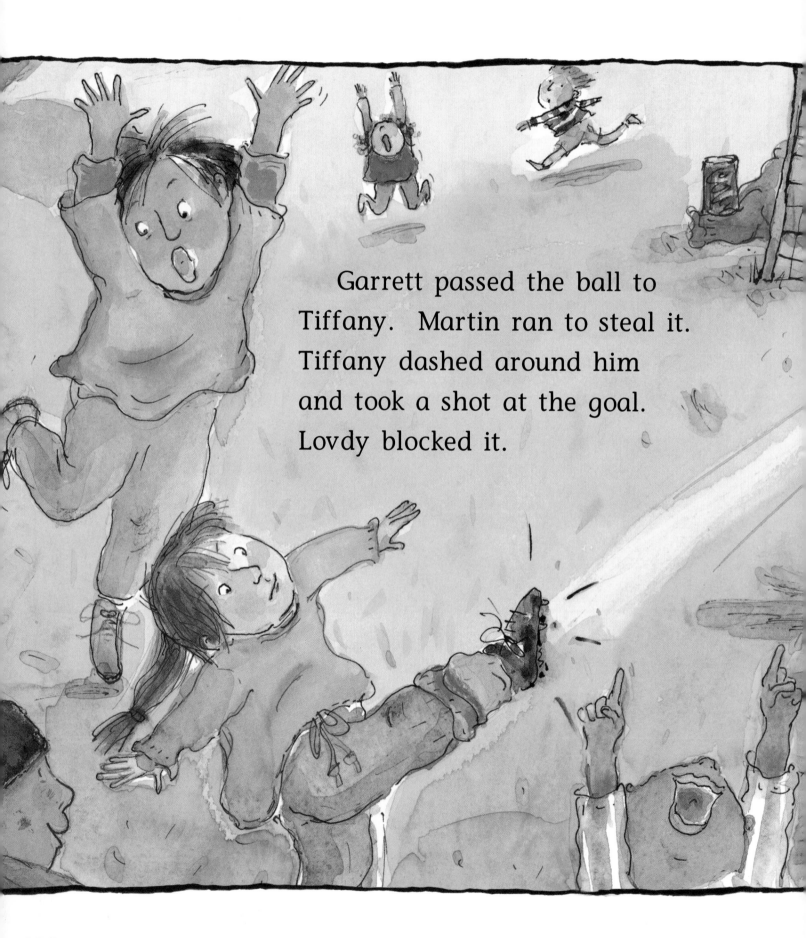

Garrett passed the ball to
Tiffany. Martin ran to steal it.
Tiffany dashed around him
and took a shot at the goal.
Lovdy blocked it.

Mia just stood
by the side and
watched.

The next day, Garrett picked Mia first for his team.

Mia got the ball. She dribbled down the field. *Smack!* She kicked the ball toward the goal.

And Lovdy caught it.

No goal.

No cheering.

"Too bad, Mia," Garrett said. "Better luck next time."

Mia felt tears in her eyes.

"She's going to quit," whispered Lovdy. "I *knew* it."

Mia still hated losing. But she didn't hate losing as much as she loved soccer.

"Ready to play?" asked Garrett.

Mia nodded.

Garrett grinned at her. He passed her the ball.

Mia ran down the field. Tap, tap, tap with her toes. The ball stayed right with her, like a friend. She got ready to kick it into the goal.

Mia kicked the ball as hard as she could.

Maybe she'd score the goal. Maybe she wouldn't.

But she was playing.

And that was more important than winning or losing . . .

because winners never quit!

Read Together

Your Turn

1. In the story, the word <u>field</u> means —

⬭ a hill

⬭ a playground

⬭ a grassy play area

TEKS 1.3H, 1.6C

2. ✔ TARGET SKILL **Understanding Characters**
How do Mia's feelings about winning change in the story? TEKS 1.4B, 1.9B, ELPS 4J

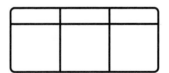

3. Oral Language Tell two things you learned about Mia. Use the Retelling Cards. TEKS 1.4B, 1.9B, 1.28

Retelling Cards

 TEKS **1.3H** identify/read high-frequency words; **1.4B** ask questions/seek clarification/locate details about texts; **1.6C** use syntax/context to determine meaning; **1.9B** describe/analyze characters; **1.24C** record information in visual formats; **1.28** share information/ideas by speaking clearly; **ELPS** **4J** employ inferential skills to demonstrate comprehension

I Read

Home at Last
by Forest Van Grant
illustrated by Kristin Barr

✓ **PHONICS SKILL**

Two-Syllable Words
Prefixes **un-, re-**

✓ **WORDS TO KNOW**

loved
everyone

 TEKS **1.3A(i)** decode words with consonants; **1.3A(ii)** decode words with vowels; **1.3C(i)** decode using closed syllables; **1.3C(ii)** decode using open syllables; **1.3E** read words with inflectional endings; **ELPS** **4A** learn English sound-letter relationships/decode

Home at Last

by Forest Von Gront

illustrated by Kristin Barr

Tony and his family were in their new home. Dad repainted Tony's new bedroom. Tony helped. Dad let Tony decide which paint he liked. Tony was glad he chose blue.

Dad unwrapped three new lights.
He replaced the old lights. Tony's
new room looked much brighter.

Then the van came at noon.
The workers quickly unloaded the
van. Everyone helped put things
where they belonged.

Tony unpacked his books. He
and Mom unpacked sheets and
made his bed. Before long, the
room started to look cozy.

Tony found his box of toys.
Then his bedroom began to look
like home. It was nice to settle in
so quickly.

Tony helped unpack dishes,
pots, and pans. Dad set up a table.
Mom, Dad, and Tony ate their first
meal in their new home.

The long day was over. There
was still a lot to do, but it felt like
home. Tony loved it! So did Mom
and Dad.

Be a Team Player

Connect to Social Studies

✔ WORDS TO KNOW

loved	sorry
everyone	only
brothers	people
field	most

GENRE

Informational text gives facts about a topic. Find facts about being on a team in this social studies text.

TEXT FOCUS

A **checklist** is a list of names or things to think about or do. What do you learn from p. 200?

TEKS **1.3E** read words with inflectional endings; **1.14B** identify important facts/details; **1.14D** use text features to locate information

Be a Team Player

Have you ever loved playing on a team? Most people have lots of fun on a team.

All kinds of people play on teams. Sisters and brothers play. Friends and cousins play.

There are all kinds of teams. Some people play baseball or basketball. Some play soccer or volleyball. People may play on a field or on a court.

No matter what kind of team it is, it's important to be a good team player. Try not to feel sorry if you lose a game. Everyone loses sometimes. It's only important to try your best and have fun.

Here is a checklist of things to remember when you play on a team.

Be a Team Player.

✔ Pay attention to the coach.

✔ Follow the rules.

✔ Do your best.

✔ Don't quit.

✔ Have fun!

Making Connections

Read Together

Text to Self

TEKS 1.18B, RC-1(F)

Poem Write a poem about a time you were on a team. Use words that tell about sights, sounds, and feelings.

Text to Text

TEKS 1.19C, RC-1(F)

Write About It Did Mia become a good team player? Tell what things about her make you think so.

Text to World

TEKS 1.4B, RC-1(F)

Connect to Health Read nonfiction books and other texts to find facts about a sport. Read carefully and look at the pictures to figure out information. Write two facts.

TEKS **1.4B** ask questions/seek clarification/locate details about texts; **1.18B** write short poems; **1.19C** write brief comments on texts; **RC-1(F)** make connections to experiences/texts/community; **ELPS 1E** internalize new basic/academic language; **3H** narrate/describe/explain with detail; **5G** narrate/describe/explain in writing

Grammar

Read Together

Adjectives That Compare Add **er** to adjectives to compare two. Add **est** to compare more than two.

Compare Two

Meg is tall<u>er</u> than Jon.

Compare More Than Two

Abe is the tall<u>est</u> goalie of all.

tall　　　**taller**　　　**tallest**

Try This!

Write adjectives from the boxes to finish the sentences. Use another sheet of paper.

small	smaller	smallest

1. We have a very __?__ soccer team.

2. Our team is the __?__ team in town.

3. Brad's team is __?__ than Eva's team.

fast	faster	fastest

4. I am __?__ than Kyla.

5. Rob is the __?__ runner in the game.

Grammar in Writing

When you revise your writing, try adding some adjectives that compare.

203

Write to Respond

Read Together

✓ **Organization** In a good **opinion paragraph**, a topic sentence tells an opinion. A closing sentence retells the opinion in new words.

Tara drafted her paragraph. Then she added a closing sentence.

Revised Draft

He looks for clues until the case is solved. ∧Inspector Hopper does the greatest job!

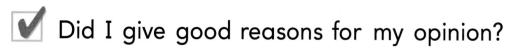

Revise Checklist

✓ Does my topic sentence tell my opinion?

✓ Did I give good reasons for my opinion?

✓ Do I need to add more examples to explain my reasons?

✓ Does my closing sentence retell my opinion?

Which sentence tells Tara's opinion? Which sentence tells it again? Now make changes to revise your draft. Use the Checklist.

Final Copy

Not a Quitter

Inspector Hopper is a very good detective. One reason is because he gets the facts. He finds out what the boat looks like. Also, he doesn't quit. He looks for clues until the case is solved. Inspector Hopper does the greatest job!

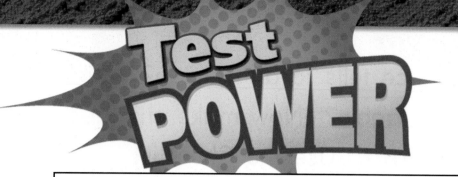

Read both stories. Then read each question.
Choose the best answer for the question.

A Good Idea

Kit was in the school play. She was happy about it. Kit was also a little scared. She studied her lines, but she did not know a lot of them.

She did not want to give up. Kit asked her brother Jay for help. Jay thought about Kit's lines. He said, "I know that learning a rhyme helps me remember things."

Kit and her brother worked together. They made up some rhymes. Soon Kit knew her lines well. Now she felt good about the play.

"You are the best, Jay!" said Kit. "You have been so <u>helpful</u>."

The First Ride

A long time ago, two brothers named Wilbur and Orville Wright built a plane. It was made of wood. The wings were made with cloth. One brother rode on a wing. He had his hands on the controls. The other brother ran next to the plane. He held on to help keep it steady.

The plane rose up. It flew for twelve seconds. This may not seem like a long time now, but it was a great time back then!

After this first flight, the brothers made more planes. They learned how to make them better. The Wright brothers helped people learn how to make and fly planes.

GO ON

1   In the story "A Good Idea," the word
helpful means —

  ⬭ worried
  ⬭ no help
  ⬭ a big help

2   How are these two stories alike?

  ⬭ They are both about people who work
  together and don't give up.
  ⬭ They are both about an airplane ride.
  ⬭ They both take place long ago.

3   How are these two stories different?

  ⬭ "The First Ride" gives facts about
  a real event.
  ⬭ The people in "A Good Idea" give up.
  ⬭ "The First Ride" is a make-believe
  story.

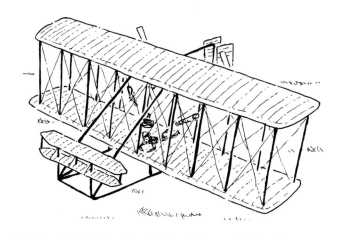

STOP

POWER Practice

TEKS **1.4B** ask questions/seek clarification/locate details about texts; **1.20C** ask questions with subject-verb inversion

Seek Clarification

When you want more information, you can ask a question. Often a question word or a verb comes first in a question. The words in the answer often use the same words in a different order.

Statement: **Jim can** paint it.

Question: What **can Jim** paint?

Answer: **Jim can** paint the box.

Read each sentence. On a sheet of paper, write a question to get more information. Be sure that your words are in an order that makes sense. Trade papers with a partner. Write answers to your partner's questions.

1. Manny was chasing them.

2. Lily was looking over there.

3. Annie is making it.

4. Dad is cooking it.

5. Arlo should pass the ball.

TEKS 1.21A form letters legibly

Handwriting

Be sure your sentences are spaced correctly. Remember to use the correct mark at the end of each sentence.

correct

Who is it? It's Jess.

too close

Whoisit?It'sJess.

too far apart

Who is it?   It's Jess.

Write these sentences on a sheet of paper.
Use your best handwriting. Use correct
spacing. Remember to use the correct mark
at the end of each sentence.

Are you ready? It's time
to go. Grab your jacket.
Hurry up!

Read your sentences to a partner.

Write your own sentence about getting
ready to go somewhere.

TEKS 1.16A recognize media purposes

Media Purposes

Read Together

Media are ways of communicating with many people. Books, magazines, TV, and the Internet are kinds of media. Different kinds of media can have different purposes. Some are for fun, and some give information.

Before you use a media source for research, think about its purpose.

• Is this magazine story written for fun, or does it give information?

• Is this website only for playing games, or does it tell facts?

If a media source gives information and facts, it is a good source for your report.

214

Work with a partner. Talk about these magazine stories and websites. Decide which ones would be good sources for a research report. Give reasons for your answers.

1.

All About Elephants

2.

Fun with Elephants

3.

Elephants in the Wild

4.

My Elephant Friend

TEKS 1.21A form letters legibly

Handwriting

Read Together

Be sure your words and sentences are spaced correctly. Remember to begin each special name with a capital letter.

correct

Where are Tess and Lucy?

too close

WhereareTessandLucy?

too far apart

Where are Tess and Lucy?

216

Write these sentences on a sheet of paper. Use your best handwriting. Use correct spacing. Begin each special name with a capital letter.

They are on the bus with Ben. Mr. Lee is driving. We are still waiting for Hanna.

Write your own sentence about a bus trip.

TEKS 1.16A recognize media purposes

Media Purposes

Read
Together

Media are ways of communicating with many people. When you do research, you can use different kinds of media to find information on your topic. You might find information by watching movies or TV shows.

Before you take notes, think about what you are watching. Was the movie or TV show made for fun, or was it made to give information? If it was made to give information, it is a good source for your report.

Talk about these movies and TV shows with your classmates. Decide which ones would be good sources for a report. Tell about your ideas. Listen to your classmates' ideas. Be sure to follow your classroom's discussion rules.

1.

2.

3.

4.

TEKS 1.16B identify media techniques

Media Techniques

A research report answers a question about a topic. You can find facts for your report in many places.

You can read books and magazines.

You can look at pictures and charts.

You can watch movies and TV shows.

When you watch a movie or a TV show, you see pictures. You see how people and animals move. You hear sounds, too. Sometimes the sounds include music. The pictures, the movement, and the sounds all give you information.

220

Talk about these pictures with your classmates. Think about what you would see and hear in a movie with each picture. What movements would you see? What sounds would you hear?

1.

2.

3.

4.

TEKS 1.27B follow/restate/give oral instructions; **ELPS 2I** demonstrate listening comprehension of spoken English

Follow Directions

Directions tell how to do something. It's important to follow the steps in order. You can follow directions. You can also give directions.

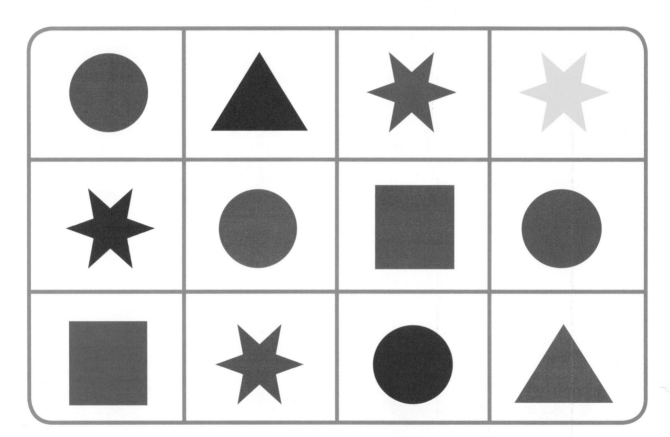

Trace the following path with your finger.

1. Start at the red circle. ●

2. Go right 2 squares. ➡

3. Go down 2 squares.

4. Go left 1 square. ⬅

5. Where did you end? ✦

Think about the directions you followed. Use your own words to give the directions to a partner. Where does your partner end?

Now make up your own directions. Tell a partner how to get from the pink triangle to another shape. Have your partner use a finger to follow your directions.
Then switch roles.
Repeat and follow
each direction your
partner gives.

TEKS 1.21A form letters legibly; 1.22D spell words with inflectional endings

Spelling

Adding **s** to most nouns makes them mean more than one.

one **dog**   three **dogs**

one **kitten**   four **kittens**

one **friend**   many **friends**

one **sister**   two **sisters**

Read each noun. Add **s** to make the word mean more than one. Write the word you make. Use your best handwriting.

1. plant

2. book

3. bike

4. lake

5. day

6. night

7. bug

8. bird

Read the words you have written.

Make up some sentences using the words you have written.

TEKS 1.26 create visual display/dramatization

Sharing Facts

Read
Together

A research report answers a question about a topic. After you find facts for your report, you should plan how you will share those facts. Here are some of the things you can do.

Make a poster.

Show an activity.

Work with a partner. Together, pick one of the how-to report topics from the next page. The facts for each report are listed. Plan a poster to show the facts.

How to Make a Celery Snack

- Wash a stick of celery.

- Spread peanut butter on it.

- Add 4 raisins on the peanut butter.

- Eat and enjoy!

How to Make a Puppet

- Draw a face on a paper plate.

- Glue a craft stick to the back of the plate.

- Hold the puppet by the stick and make it talk.

Work together to draw the poster you planned.

Now plan how you will show the activity you chose. With your partner, practice showing the activity.

Share your how-to posters with the rest of the class.

TEKS 1.16B identify media techniques

Media Techniques

Read Together

A research report answers a question about a topic. You can find facts for your report in many places.

You might get information from a movie or a TV show. When you do, you see pictures. You may see how people and animals move. You hear sounds, too. Sometimes you hear music. The pictures, movement, sounds, and music all give you information.

Talk about these pictures with a partner. What kind of music do you think you would hear in a movie with each picture? Would the music be fast or slow? Would it make you feel happy or sad? Share your ideas with your partner.

1.

2.

3.

4.

TEKS 1.8 respond to/use rhythm/rhyme/alliteration

Poetry

Listen to this poem.

> Swish, swoosh. Swish, swoosh.
>
> It sounds right—I hope.
>
> Swish, swoosh. Swish, swoosh.
>
> At last I'm jumping rope!

What rhyming words do you hear?

Which words begin with the same sound?

Clap the rhythm as you read the poem again.

These pictures might give you ideas for other poems. Write your own short poem. Use some rhyming words. Use words that begin with the same sound. When you are finished, say your poem and clap out the rhythm.

TEKS 1.20A(iv) understand/use adverbs

Adverbs

Remember that an **adverb** tells more about a verb.

My dog barks.
<u>How</u> does it bark?
My dog barks **loudly**.

Adverbs			
How	**Where**	**When**	**How Much**
loudly	up	first	very
softly	down	next	too
quickly	inside	today	so
slowly	outside	yesterday	completely
proudly	here	before	hardly
carefully	there	after	almost

Choose an adverb to complete each sentence.
Say the sentence. Then write it.

1. He reads _____ lunch. (before, after)

2. I read my book _____. (quickly, carefully)

3. They play _____. (outside, inside)

4. We run _____ the hill. (up, down)

5. We talk _____ fast. (very, too)

Work with a partner. Choose other adverbs to
complete the sentences. Say and write them.

TEKS **1.21A** form letters legibly; **1.22C** spell high-frequency words

Spelling

Read Together

Read the words. Then answer the questions on another sheet of paper.

almost	happened	idea	leaves
high	always	gone	across
behind	any	hello	stories

1. Which four words begin with **a**?

2. Which two words end in **d**?

3. Which word is another way of saying **hi**?

4. Which word is the opposite of **low**?

Handwriting  Read Together

Write each word neatly on a sheet of paper.
Check that the letters are formed correctly.

1. idea

2. leaves

3. gone

4. stories

Try This!

Write a sentence using two words from
the box on page 234.

TEKS **1.26** create visual display/dramatization

Sharing Facts

A research report answers a question about a topic. You can share your report with your classmates in different ways.

Draw a graph.

Act out a skit.

When you draw a graph, you use shapes, pictures, numbers, and words to share information. Be sure your graph is big and neat, so everyone can understand your report.

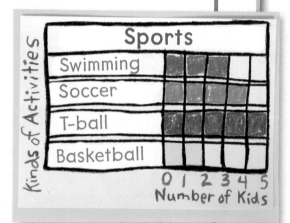

Discuss the Favorite Sports chart on the next page with a group. The numbers show how many people like each sport. Plan a graph that will show these facts.

Favorite Sports

swimming	3
soccer	12
T-ball	8
basketball	1

Work together to draw the graph you planned.

Now work together to plan a skit that will report your facts. Practice the skit together. Share your graph and your skit with the rest of your classmates.

TEKS 1.17E publish/share writing

Publishing  Read Together

After you wrote your opinion paragraph, you revised it. Now you are ready to share your paragraph with the rest of your class.

One way to share your paragraph is to read it out loud. These tips will help you read your paragraph well.

- Practice reading your paragraph.
- Speak slowly.
- Use a loud, clear voice.

Work with a group of classmates. Together, talk about each paragraph. Be sure it is as good as it can be. Share your ideas, and listen to each other. Remember to follow your classroom's discussion rules.

Write a neat copy of your paragraph.

Then work with a partner. Take turns reading your paragraphs out loud. Practice reading slowly and clearly. Help your partner do a good job.

After you have practiced, read your paragraph to your whole class.

Make a book of opinion paragraphs. Put your group's paragraphs together. Work together to make a cover for your book. Add the book to your classroom library.

OUR CLASS OPINIONS

TEKS 1.21A form letters legibly; **1.22C** spell high-frequency words

Spelling  Read Together

Read the words. Then answer the questions on another sheet of paper.

brothers	different	field	loved
happy	people	ball	most
only	everyone	sorry	large

1. Which four words have double letters?

2. Which two words end like **jelly**?

3. Which word means **big**?

4. Which word is a compound word?

Handwriting Read Together

Write each word neatly on a sheet of paper. Check that the letters are formed correctly.

1. brothers

2. people

3. most

4. only

Try This!

Write a silly story. See how many words from the box you can use in your story. Remember to begin each sentence with a capital letter.

TEKS **1.26** create visual display/dramatization

Sharing Facts

Read Together

A research report answers a question about a topic. Once you have facts about your topic, you can share your report with your classmates. You could make a big book or a poster. You could also act out a skit.

Plan your own research reports. Think of a topic or choose one of these topics.

taking care of a pet

how to make a cake

a firefighter's job

Now use sources to find information about your topic. You might use books, magazines, websites, and other sources. You might also interview people about your topic.

Take notes on the facts you find. Write only the most important facts you read and hear. If you use a book, do not copy from it. Write in your own words.

Plan and make a big book or a poster to share the facts you found. Show your big book or poster to your classmates.

Now plan a skit that will share the facts you found. Ask one or two classmates to help you put on your skit. Practice your words and actions together. Then act out your skit for the rest of your classmates.

Remember these helpful tips when you plan your skit.

- Plan what you will say.

- Practice your words and movements.

- Speak slowly.

- Use a loud, clear voice.

- Use large, clear movements.

Words to Know

Unit 6   High-Frequency Words

26 The Dot

teacher	bear
studied	above
surprised	even
toward	pushed

27 What Can You Do?

different	high
near	always
enough	once
stories	happy

28 "The Kite"

second	heard
ball	large
across	cried
head	should

29 "A Boat Disappears"

leaves	hello
any	behind
happened	idea
gone	almost

30 Winners Never Quit!

loved	sorry
everyone	only
brothers	people
field	most

Glossary

A

already

Already means before this. My brother was **already** at school by the time my bus arrived.

anyway

Anyway means that something doesn't matter. Mia had a sore foot, but she went to school **anyway**.

B

binoculars

Binoculars are something you look through to make things look closer. Seth looked through the **binoculars** and saw an eagle in a tree.

blank

Blank means with no writing on it. The sheet of paper was **blank**.

C

captain

A **captain** is a kind of leader. Suzie is the **captain** of our swim team.

computers

A **computer** is a machine that works with words, pictures, and numbers. We have two **computers** in our classroom.

D

disappeared

To **disappear** means to stop being seen. The sun **disappeared** behind a cloud.

dribbled

To **dribble** means to use your hands or feet to move a ball from one place to another. Brian **dribbled** the ball past the other players.

F

float

To **float** means to move on top of water. I like to **float** on a raft in the pool.

G

gazing

To **gaze** means to look at something. When Ms. Tam found Ben, he was **gazing** out the window.

goalie

A **goalie** is the player who tries to keep the other team from scoring points. Lupe is the best **goalie** on our soccer team.

H

helpful

To be **helpful** means to help someone do something. I like to be **helpful** by setting the table for dinner.

I

inspector

An **inspector** is someone who looks into things. The **inspector** asked the woman questions about her lost bag.

J

junk

Junk is something that people do not want. Max and his mom took the **junk** out with the rest of the trash.

L

laughter

Laughter is what you hear when people think something is funny. The story was so funny that we all burst into **laughter**.

N

noticed
To **notice** is to see or hear something. Jason **noticed** the spot on his shirt.

P

perhaps
Perhaps means maybe. **Perhaps** our class will go there on a field trip.

R

rather
Rather is used when you like one thing more than another. I would **rather** ride a bike than walk.

S

sailed
To **sail** means to move on water in a boat. We quickly **sailed** past the other boats.

solved

To **solve** means to find the answer to a problem. Our class **solved** the problem together.

something

Something means any thing. I wanted to wear **something** red that day.

squiggle

A **squiggle** is a wavy line. My little brother made a **squiggle** with the red crayon.

straight

If something is **straight**, it has no turns or curves. I used a ruler to make my lines **straight**.

swirly

Swirly means in a curving way. Lily used a brush to make **swirly** blue lines on her painting.

Y

yummy

If something is **yummy**, that means it tastes good. That strawberry is **yummy!**

Acknowledgments

"A Boat Disappears" from *Inspector Hopper* by Doug Cushman. Copyright © **2000** by Doug Cushman. All rights reserved. Reprinted by permission of HarperCollins Children's Books, a division of HarperCollins Publishers.

"Caracol, caracol/To a Snail" from *¡Pío Peep!: Traditional Spanish Nursery Rhymes*, selected by Alma Flor Ada & F. Isabel Campoy. Spanish compilation copyright © **2003** by Alma Flor Ada & Isabel Campoy. English adaptation copyright © **2003** by Alice Schertle. Reprinted by permission of HarperCollins Publishers.

Days with Frog and Toad by Arnold Lobel. Copyright © **1979** by Arnold Lobel. All rights reserved. Reprinted by permission of HarperCollins Children's Books, a division of HarperCollins Publishers.

The Dot by Peter H. Reynolds. Copyright © **2003** by Peter H. Reynolds. Reprinted by permission of the publisher Candlewick Press Inc. and Pippin Properties, Inc.

"Song of the Bugs" from *Nibble, Nibble* by Margaret Wise Brown. Copyright © **1959** by William R. Scott, Inc., renewed **1987** by Roberta Brown Rauch. Reprinted by permission of HarperCollins Publishers.

What Can You Do? by Shelley Rotner and Sheila Kelley, with photographs by Shelley Rotner. Coauthor of text and photographs copyright © **2001** by Shelley Rotner. Coauthor of text copyright © **2001** by Sheila Kelley. Reprinted by the permission of Millbrook Press, a division of Lerner Publishing Group. Inc. All rights reserved.

Winners Never Quit! by Mia Hamm, illustrated by Carol Thompson. Text and illustrations copyright © **2004** by Mia Hamm and Byron Preiss Visual Publications, Inc. All rights reserved. Reprinted by permission of HarperCollins Children's Books, a division of HarperCollins Publishers.

"Worm" from *A Little Book of Little Beasts* by Mary Ann Hoberman. Copyright © **1973,** renewed 2001 by Mary Ann Hoberman. Reprinted by permission of Gina Maccoby Literary Agency.

Credits